IN GOD'S SHADOW

'ABDU'L-BAHÁ

AND THE INCARNATION
OF THE IDEAL

| Shahbaz Fatheazam |

*To Dr. Iraj Ayman,
a kinship in letters, my abiding gratitude.*

INDEX

PART ONE

PAST & PRESENT

Haifa, Palestine, Mout Carmel circa 1888

When 'Abdu'l-Bahá[1] passed away in Haifa, Palestine, in the early hours of November 28, 1921, a philosophically skeptical and painfully realistic Age of Anxiety had established itself.

---

[1] Birth name Abbas Effendi, born May 23rd 1844, and the eldest son of Bahá'u'lláh, prophet founder of the Bahá'í Faith. The title 'Abdu'l-Bahá (or Servant of the Glory) was adopted after the ascension of Bahá'u'lláh in 1892.

The world was uncertain and afraid, unsettled and incendiary. A rapidly changing landscape was to sweep it. One French essayist and philosopher, writing within a year after the passing of 'Abdu'l-Bahá, summed it up well: *"We think of what has disappeared, and we are almost destroyed by what has been destroyed, we do not know what will be born, and we fear the future, not without reason. We hope vaguely, we dread precisely, our fears are infinitely more precise than our hopes, we confess that the charm of life is behind us... but doubt and disorder are in us and with us. There is no thinking man... who can hope to dominate his anxiety to escape from this impression of darkness... But among all these injured things is the Mind... it passes a mournful judgment on itself. It doubts itself profoundly."*[1]

'Abdu'l-Bahá's Ministry (1892-1921) was unique as it stood at the confluence of three lost generations, hearts torn, voices hoarse, and with eyes so used to darkness that they had become unable to tell candlelight from sunlight.

The first such lost generation had initiated into the world unfit to live normal lives dragged as it was into the battlefields and bayonets of war, struggling to fall or die on slippery, blood soaked trenches dug in zigzag patterns stretching frontiers from the Belgian Coast to the Swiss border, with enemy trenches generally only 500 yards apart. We are, of course, referring to the

---

[1] Paul Valéry, in his address delivered at the University of Zurich on November 15th, 1922, quoted *in Sources of European History Since 1900*, 2nd Edition, by Marvin Perry, Matthew Berg, and James Krukones, Wadsworth Cengage Learning, Boston, 2011, page 78.

First World War (1914-1918) where returning to normality was seen as a rude betrayal of the experience of horror or of comradeship amidst the horror and the men and women involved preferred to be lost to themselves and to the world rather than betray what was undoubtedly and miserably their own.[1]

First World War

This embattled cohort was to be followed immediately by two more such 'lost generations': the second, born about ten years later, in the first decades of the twentieth century, was

---

[1] With entire nations armed, "the spirit of ruthless brutality [would] enter into the very fiber of…national life…" [Woodrow Wilson, quoted in Prologue Magazine, **America Enters the Great War,** Spring 2017, Vol. 49, No. 1]. The monumental battles of 1914, 1915, and 1916, especially Second Ypres, Tannenberg, Verdun, and the Somme, attained a level of destructiveness and horror never before experienced in war. The Battle of the Somme, which began on July 1, 1916, claimed nearly a million killed, wounded and missing by the time it was over in mid-November. Nearly ten million died in the Great War and an additional twenty-one million were wounded, crippled, blinded, or otherwise impaired.

taught the overwhelming lessons of hyperinflation[1], mass unemployment, revolutionary unrest and the instability of whatever had been left intact in Europe after four years of slaughter; the third, again born ten years later, had the bitter choice of initiating the world by Nazi concentration camps, the Spanish Civil War, and the Moscow trials, the latter setting the stage for the great purges which occurred during Stalin's Soviet Union in the 1930s.

Nazi Concentration Camps

---

[1] Inflation is a monetary phenomenon but hyperinflation is always and everywhere a political phenomenon. It cannot occur without a fundamental malfunction of a country's political economy. One way of understanding the post-war hyperinflation is to see it as a form of state bankruptcy. See Niall Ferguson, *The Ascent of Money: A Financial History of the World*, Penguin Press, New York, 2008, pages 102-104.

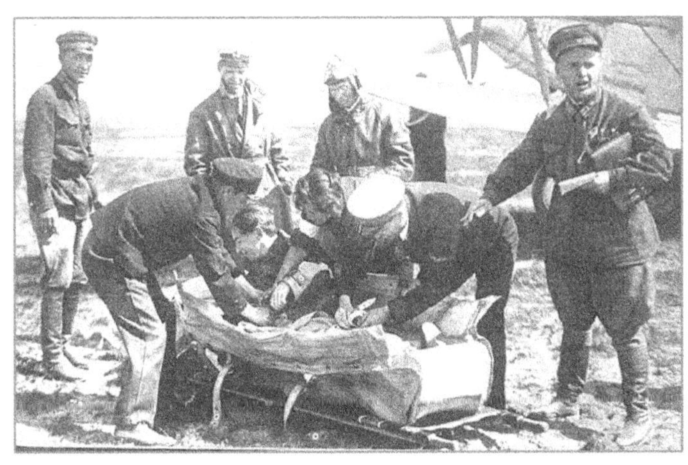

Spanish Civil War

These three groups are close enough to form one weightless race of men in a wasted world that was supposed to house them – a weightlessness that condemned them to irrelevance.[1] Sequestered and sullied, all three generations suffered the breaking of all social bonds and all time becoming time present. Both hope in the future and love to the past erased. Worse than to die is to live with a memory which serves no purpose.

---

[1] One obscure member of the lost generation, a wounded German soldier, became its voice: "I am young, I am twenty years old; yet I know nothing of life but despair, death, fear and fatuous superficiality cast over an abyss of sorrow. I see how peoples are set against one another, and in silence, unknowingly, foolishly, obediently, innocently slay one another…What do they expect of us if a time ever comes when the war is over? Through the years our business has been killing – it was our first calling in life. Our knowledge of life is limited to death. What will happen afterwards? And what shall come out of us?" Quoted *in **Sources of European History Since 1900**, 2nd Edition, by Marvin Perry, Matthew Berg, and James Krukones, Wadsworth Cengage Learning, Boston, 2011, page 79.

When the Treaty of Versailles, together with its 440 articles, was signed in Paris in the summer of 1919, exactly five years after the assassination of Archduke Franz Ferdinand, dwarf statesmen despairingly scrambled through the thick smoke to build on a broken peace.

Treaty of Versailles

The Treaty had set its eyes on the self-improvement of nations. But the self-interest of press-applauded, vengeful public figures[1] was discreetly veiled by a façade of self-determination which in and of itself was untenable. Economic volatility was omnipresent, the ghost of multi-ethnic communities made

---

[1] One British Treasury's principal representative at the peace conference at Versailles wrote of the French Prime Minister, Georges Clemenceau: *"He had one illusion – France; and one disillusion, mankind."* John Maynard Keynes, quoted in **The Life of John Maynard Keynes**, by R.F. Harrod, 1951, page 257.

national boundaries meaningless[1] and empires, hitherto bastions of stability for their hegemony, had crumbled. Political systems, centuries in the building, had come apart – sometimes in a matter of days. The German authoritarian monarchy had become a parliamentary republic in nine days; the Tsarist empire was overtaken by a Communist republic in nine months, on February 1917; the German empire had disappeared, the Austro-Hungarian empire, with its entangled ten different languages, was broken, the Russian and Ottoman empires were swallowed. The swirling dust of cobwebbed kingdoms and humbled monarchies had made mankind unable to see itself in any other way but as an island besieged, unglued, and safety hopeless.

'Abdu'l-Bahá recognized the dangers inherent in instability as old as historical experience itself (here I am reminded of the angel's eerie cry of warning on a parchment transcribed two years before the historic Peace of Westphalia in 1648 ending Thirty Years of devastating conflict involving most of Europe which read: *"Should the madding world not betake itself to peace a weighty punishment shall it face."*)[2] And now 'Abdu'l-Bahá wrote revealingly in January 1919, two days before the impossible Paris Peace Conference was convened: *"Although the*

---

[1] At the time of the signing of the Treaty of Versailles only 65% of the population of Poland were Polish, just over half of the population of the independent country of Czechoslovakia, formed as a result of the critical intervention of U.S. President Woodrow, were Czech, and the ruling Serbs of Yugoslavia were a significant minority given that they constituted 44% of the population.

[2] Cited by Cambridge historian, Christopher M. Clark, in his documentary, ***Religion, Beliefs, and Ideas: The Story of Europe, Part 2***
https://www.youtube.com/watch?v=SMK2giWc9oI

representatives of various governments are assembled in Paris in order to lay the foundations of Universal Peace and thus bestow rest and comfort upon the world of humanity, yet misunderstanding among some individuals is still predominant and self-interest still prevails. In such an atmosphere, Universal Peace will not be practicable, nay rather, fresh difficulties will arise."[1] A year later, He continued in deliberate prescient tone: "*... in the future another war, fiercer than the last, will assuredly break out. Verily of this there is no doubt whatever.*"[2]

The social panorama in the latter years of 'Abdu'l-Bahá was undergoing massive change. One eminent historian went as far as to label it as the Age of Catastrophe.[3] Capital intensive and labor saving technology was rapidly displacing or replacing workers with a course no one could foresee, a result no one could foretell with other decisive changes coming in those years immediately after First World War. The more complex the technology, that is, the more complex the process from discovery to production, the harder to pin the benefits against the externalities, either in planning and organizing the resources as in mobilizing them. The dehumanizing effects of poverty, the multiple consequences of economic injustice, and the institutionalized nature of class inequality were emerging as

---

[1] This comes from a Tablet of 'Abdu'l-Bahá to a friend in Portland, Oregon, on January 10, 1919, two days before the conference convened. Refer to the book by Alan Ward, ***239 Days: 'Abdu'l-Bahá's Journey in America***, published in 1979 by the US Baha'i Publishing Trust, (Day 231).
[2] Ibid.
[3] Eric Hobsbawm, from his book, ***The Age of Extremes: A History of the World, 1914–1991*** (New York: Pantheon, 1995).

obsessions alongside the subtle nuances of accelerating technological and industrial advances, happening year after year.

The proud display of international expositions both sides of the Atlantic, the first manned flight (1903), the moving assembly line established in 1913, the motor car, the talkies and so many other astonishing feats in the arts and sciences, shattered old world views. These achievements transformed everyday life in both rich and poor countries, and brought in its wake burning political and moral questions of redistribution.[1]

In these vertigo years, it is ironic to see how aristocrats and capitalists, at the time, felt secure in their positions and how socialists felt certain of their chimeric faith.

Into this hardened shell of distorted economics 'Abdu'l-Bahá breathed life by transforming it, applying the spiritual to the material: *"... each member of the body politic should live in the utmost comfort and welfare because each individual member of humanity is a member of the body politic and if one member of*

---

[1] Tracking the share of over-all income taken by the top ten per cent of households in the United States alone from 1910 to 2010 the chart would center on a U shape. Inequality climbed steeply in the Roaring Twenties, and then falls sharply in the decade and a half following the Great Crash of October, 1929. From the mid-forties to the mid-seventies, the tendency is one of stability and then the chart takes off, eventually topping the 1928 level in 2007. Refer to the ambitious book about rising inequality by French economist Thomas Piketty, **Capital in the Twenty-first Century,** Harvard University Press, 2014. Piketty in his book exposes capitalism's 'central contradiction': the rate of return on capital **(r)** exceeds the rate of economic growth **(g)** and inequality tends to rise because profits and other types of income from capital tend to grow faster than wage income, which is what most people everywhere rely on. 'Patrimonial capitalism', as he puts it, is generating vast distortions in wealth concentration.

the members be in distress or be afflicted with some disease all the other members must necessarily suffer. For example, a member of the human organism is the eye. If the eye should be affected that affliction would affect the whole nervous system. Hence, if a member of the body politic becomes afflicted, in reality, from the standpoint of sympathetic connection, all will share that affliction since this (one afflicted) is a member of the group of members, a part of the whole. Is it possible for one member or part to be in distress and the other members to be at ease? It is impossible! Hence God has desired that in the body politic of humanity each one shall enjoy perfect welfare and comfort."[1]

John Keynes

Such an allusion to a divine economy could not be discarded as sentimental utopia. No less than the prominent economist, John Keynes, already writing and publishing at the time of

---

[1] 'Abdu'l-Bahá, *Foundations of World Unity*, Wilmette: Bahá'í Publishing Trust, 1979, page 38.

'Abdu'l-Bahá, famously stated: *"The ideas of economists and political philosophers… are more powerful than is commonly understood. Indeed, the world is ruled by little else."*[1]

The Bahá'í philosophy and its direct teachings on economics provided compelling validity in the early stirrings of the twentieth century, chiefly principal among them, that man's material activities must be imbued with a sense of spiritual purpose and moral obligation.

The idea is not new, but the Bahá'í formulation of it is, with its emphasis on service to humanity. [2]

Literature, in the years preceding the passing of the Master [3], was immersed in nihilism, a school of thought where the idea of

---

[1] John Maynard Keynes, **The General Theory of Employment, Interest and Money**, ch. 24, p. 383 (1935).

[2] Since the beginning of their discipline economists have devoted their energies to the underlying ethical and moral issues of human endeavour. Adam Smith set the tone for the discipline in his **Theory of Moral Sentiments** (1790) writing: "And hence it is, that to feel much for others and little for ourselves, that to restrain our selfish, and to indulge our benevolent affections, constitutes the perfection of human nature; and can alone produce among mankind that harmony of sentiments and passions in which consists their whole grace and propriety." Theory of Moral Sentiments, Part I, Of the Propriety of Action, Section I, Chapter V, § 5.

[3] The title of Master or Áqá in Farsi was given to 'Abdu'l-Bahá by His father in the Adrianople exile years (Edirne, in today's Turkey). The journey to Adrianople, according to historical accounts, *"…was the most terrible experience of travel by far. It was the beginning of winter, and very cold; heavy snow fell most of the time; and destitute as we were of proper clothing or food, it was a miracle that we survived it. We arrived at Adrianople all sick - even the young and strong. My brother again had his feet frozen on this journey."* From the sister of 'Abdu'l-Bahá, quoted in Myron Henry Phelps and Bahiyyih Khánum, **Life and Teachings of Abbas Effendi**, p. 34-36 (out of print).

decay and morbid fascinations tried desperately to express comfort in an uncomfortable situation, all the while finding it hard to ignore the invective. Prose and poems seemed to have been written only for the sake of the hopeless. Franz Kafka, a Prague born German speaking novelist who died only a few years after 'Abdu'l-Bahá's passing, and considered by many as speaking the purest German prose of the twentieth century, epitomizes this feeling of despair born in the entrapment of grotesque unreality: *"One of the first signs of the beginning of understanding is the wish to die. This life appears unbearable, another unattainable.*

Franz Kafka

One is no longer ashamed of wanting to die; one asks to be moved from the old cell, which one hates, to a new one, which one will only in time come to hate."[1]

---

[1] Quoted in **Zürau Aphorisms**, (German: *Die Zürauer Aphorismen*), a collection of 109 aphorisms by Franz Kafka, written from September 1917 to April 1918 and published by his friend Max Brod in 1931, after his death.

William Butler Yeats

'*The Second Coming*,' published in 1920 by the Nobel laureate and Irish poet William Butler Yeats, was a frightening poem. Yeats was surrounded by death. World War 1 was over, but not its terrible consequences.

The Russian Revolution shook the world order. An Irish rebellion for independence from the British was crushed. And the Spanish Flu pandemic of 1918 and 1919 had killed nearly 100 million. Along with war, unrest, and disease, this poem evokes anxiety concerning the social ills of modernity: the rupture of traditional family and societal structures;[1] the loss of collective religious faith, and with it, the collective

---

[1] The reader may well refer to a widely appealing and earnest missive of the Universal House of Justice, dated March 19th, 2025, expounding on the family unit as the basic building of community and how civilization is only able to flourish by applying a mature conception of family. The world is shaped by no less an influence of this single, dominant force. *"A family is a nation in miniature"*, 'Abdu'l-Bahá forewarns.

sense of purpose; the feeling that the old rules no longer apply and there's nothing to replace them.

Is not the "dis-ease" that surrounded the time a repeated image to the angst we feel today? It is not just human relationships and politics that are dissembling but the cosmos itself, with the ravages of climate change and pollution threatening existential chaos.

The Russian Revolution

The reason the poem *'The Second Coming,'* has been so often quoted is that everything seems to be falling apart from time to time somewhere in the world. But even historians feel like this time is different. The poem begins with the image of a falcon rising in the air in a widening spiral—soon so high and so wide that it can no longer hear the falconer. Yeats broadens the image to the world. The center can't hold, and anarchy is loosed like a blood-dimmed tide that drowns everything that is innocent. Good people are silent and the worst people get all the attention. None assumes any responsibility for action nor accountability for omission, impetuous as loitering dwellers of *homo abyssus,* 'Man's Infernal Pit'.

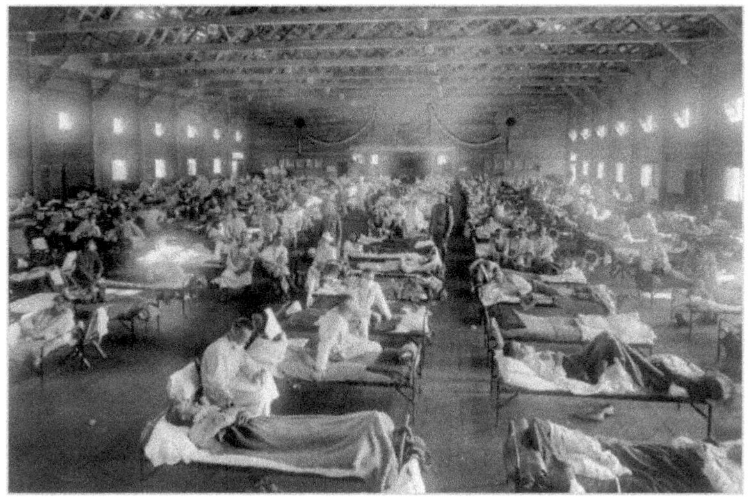

Spanish Flu

A year after 'Abdu'l-Bahá's passing, the modernist text of the famous poem by T.S. Eliot, *The Waste Land* (1922), as adumbrated by its title, alludes to the death of culture and the misery of being learned in a world that has largely forgotten its roots.

The poem of 434 lines even begins with the recurring imagery of death. T.S. Eliot made of the cacophonies of his generation a music of despair, searching for order in an anarchic world.[1]

"... Son of man,
you cannot say, or guess, for you know only a
heap of broken images, where the sunbeats, and the dead tree
gives no shelter, the cricket no relief, and the dry stone no
sound of water. "[2]

---

[1] To this we may also add James Joyce's novel **Ulysses** (first published a few months after 'Abdu'l-Bahá's passing, on February 2nd, 1922). Both books were like nothing quite seen before, in their style, scale and ambition. But also in chaos. If the world had become chaotic and unsettling, went the reasoning, than writing must be too. These two artists of modernism – the rejection of traditional linear storytelling and the use of more challenging styles to reflect the new world - remade their work: a way of seeking either to control the strange and uncontrollable, or simply to portray it more truthfully. Listed, rather dubiously, as the greatest novel of the 20th century, in James Joyce's Ulysses objects are robbed of their "aura" in the age of mechanical reproduction, and history is described in materialist terms, as a "pile of debris." In the absence of aura, everything is transformed into a fetish, a busy impulse to caress, collect, and consume. Is Ulysses really a bricolage of banality and triviality, which collects and reuses the detritus of culture and capital?

[2] T.S. Eliot, **The Waste Land**, New York, Boni & Liveright, 1922, pages 10-11

This minuscule and meager historical meditation shows the early years of the twentieth century engulfed in a breakdown of tradition, a point of no return, the persistent theme being barbarism (TS Eliot's "I had not thought death had undone so many" comes to mind), crisis and the decline of civilization. Denatured by crass materialism can humanity's bones be reassembled and animated again, in a form that can be lived with?

Politically, the downfall of the nation state; socially, the transformation of class systems into a mass society and spiritually, in the rise of nihilism.[1]   Where, O where merciful

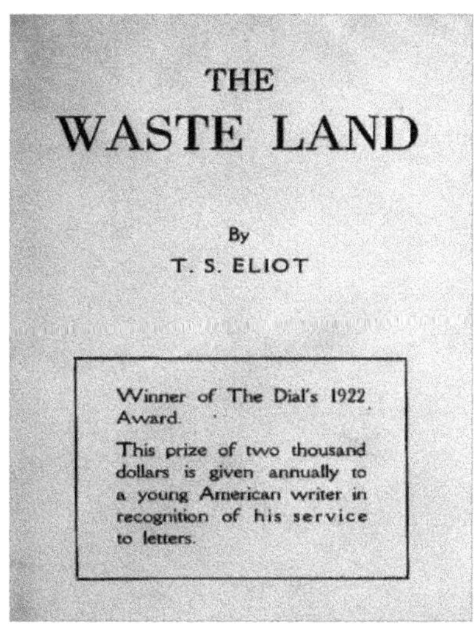

First published 1922

---

[1] Arnold Toynbee, in his monumental six volume, *A Study of History*, 1952, combines these disruptive elements for his diagnosis of the death of civilizations which he invariably sees as *"either war or class or some combination of the two"*.

Providence to pass "the sponge of oblivion across much that is suffered."

Buried has been a double skepticism. Great as have been the traumas and convulsions of the twentieth century, the disillusionment with the fundamental Enlightenment belief in progress itself as well as the faith which it rehearsed, the unshakeable belief in secular human reason, is the more insidious and harmful. The last one hundred years has thrown out the last two-hundred years of political history and the Enlightenment itself, that period in which it seemed that the advance of reason and the movement of history both pointed to social changes that would bring about freer and more just societies in the future. It seems the exercise of linking morality with reason has exhausted itself. To assume moral responsibility by a reflexive and rationally oriented human community has moved us away from our historical roots and has become even dangerous. Is not the attempt by humanity to 'purify' moral action from its religious dependency another version of the concept of "the Death of God"[1]? The detachment of moral self-determination from revealed religion and central authority is the other great uncertainty. While humanity annihilates God or seeks to develop an abstraction of God, can we place holiness in the pigeonhole of

---

[1] It was Nietzsche who popularized the concept "death of God, in 1882. He writes, *"God is dead! God remains dead! And we have killed him!"* (**Gay Science**, in the original, *Die fröhliche Wissenschaft,* page 125). While many may interpret this as a defense of atheism it is better and more completely understood as his somber diagnosis of modernity. Nietzsche regards our age as one of transition – the confluence between a period that was and a period that points ahead. For millennia, God was a living presence in our lives – today he is dead and nihilism reigns.

pure intellect? In its place we find a disturbing postmodernist disillusionment which rejects any attempt to provide a systematic explanation of the course of modern world history, discrediting all grand narratives and a retreat from all universalist forms, the socialist kind included, of political commitment, now regarded as inherently oppressive.

Implicit in any assertion of this era is the belief that this "modern" age of the Enlightenment is now passed. Is not the whole posture of linked skepticism and defeatism a symptom of intellectual and political disorientation? [1] A sign of the times, indeed, and with no basis for understanding them.

---

[1] We are reminded of G.K Chesterton, a contemporary of 'Abdu'l-Bahá, and his pithy aphorism: *"Poetry is sane because it floats easily in an infinite sea; reason seeks to cross the infinite sea, and so make it finite. The result is mental exhaustion."* From his book, ***Orthodoxy,*** page 11.

The problems which humanity faces at the centenary of 'Abdu'l-Bahá's passing are daunting; but they are not unrecognizable. This is no time, therefore, for epistemological skepticism and civic disengagement.[1]

All scenes are to drop at once upon a hundred thousand stages. And while faded order and its twin shadow disorder and past structures and modes of thought continue to be recognized as wholly inadequate and while we may pity the plumage we cannot forget or ignore the dying bird.

The dulled voices of *a perplexed and sorrowful age*[2] when 'Abdu'l-Bahá passed away are today met by a world no less disenchanted. The war generation, the generation of anger, is today's generation of languor, dire and doleful. In our time of peace, the 'pity of War' has been transformed into the pity of

---

[1] The latter is not to be confused with political action or participation in politics to push for social change to benefit one group of people over another. Community engagement naturally heightens social consciousness but this should not be misconstrued as political engagement. Politics is only one aspect of the broader phenomenon of human socioeconomic development. Economic growth, social mobilization and the power of ideas concerning justice and prosperity form an integral part of this greater context and which, to Baháís, includes the spiritual education of all members of the population – adults, youth and children. The individual's involvement in political matters is prohibited in the Baháí Faith"...*because the Cause of God is withdrawn entirely from political affairs; the political realm pertains only to the Rulers of those matters: it has nothing to do with the souls who are exerting their utmost energy to harmonizing affairs, helping character and inciting (the people) to strive for perfections. Therefore no soul is allowed to interfere with (political) matters...*" 'Abdu'l-Bahá, Bahá'í World Faith, p. 407.

[2] Quoted in the account written by Shoghi Effendi and Lady Blomfield two months after His passing, entitled, simply, ***The Passing of 'Abdu'l-Bahá***, published by Rosenfeld Bros., Haifa, 1922.

'lies and lethargies'.[1] We can neither lie still, nor sit straight, nor stand erect, much less to lean and to kneel, nor do anything but wallow. The ideas infiltrating World War I – nationalism, rule by the people, rule of international law, the rights of nations – still guide us today but more as an illusion of a hallucinatory era. Nationalism, this modern manifestation of the herd-instinct, this unreality of grouping, 'the nightmare of the nations'[2], 'a terrible enemy to civility'[3], a disease undermining even the best constitutions, and …a bogey (none can really tell what precisely a nation is), continues to push the world in the direction of territorial expansion and ideological cause, conflict and war.[4] Exhilarating and unusual recoveries do happen but are fast, furious and fragile. We live in repeated states of grace and concomitant circumstance but allow disgrace to displace them,

---

[1] The words are inspired as much by war poet Wilfred Owen's famous remark written in unfinished condition for the preface to his posthumous collection *Poems* (1920) 'My subject is…the pity of War' as by Auden's line 'Lies and lethargies police the world/In its periods of peace.' taken from his last book-length poem, *The Age of Anxiety*, published in 1947.

[2] Ascribed to as such by the historian Eric Hobsbawm in his book, *The Age of Capitalism* (1975).

[3] A description used by Clive Bell in his Essay, *Civilization* (1928).

[4] A sense of identity among peoples is a paramount feature of humanity since the dawn of time but this inherent need does not necessarily have to translate itself in political statehood. Unity on the cultural plane seldom leads to unity on the political plane and the replacement of the separate countries with a single state, the European Union for example, is not unpredictable given that such a union of member states brings with it political unity especially after a breakdown of civilization and warfare. Progress and stability can be reinstated by a universal order. Refer to Arnold Toynbee's six volume, *A Study of History*, 1952, Part V, The Disintegration of Civilizations, Chapter 32, Universal States: Ends or Means.

repeatedly. It is pride that lies awake too weak to stir even the emboldened amongst us.

The perch of modernity and ingenuity in 'Abdu'l-Bahá's time is now unhinged. Modernity is a light which obscures everything, bringing with it anxiety similar to the unexplained angst which clouded the horizon in the early part of the last century. The dark collective psyche today spurs a nomadic

(Reproduced with the kind permission of Princeton University Press. Cover of the book "The Age of Anxiety: A Baroque Eclogue by W. H. Auden. © 2011)

condition, as humanity wanders, a bit like Cain expulsed from the family's womb and cursed to eternal meandering, or Noah who is purged from humanity's sinful condition and is cleansed in baptismal banishment. Mankind's labyrinthine and erring course, its 'melancholy haphazardness'[1] prevail precisely because we have not mastered the past. Nostalgia, the soul's lament for a past denied it, persists because we continue small and yet boast greatness in mind "…*lord and master of all things, yet scarce can command anything*"[2]. It is not nature that humans cannot command, but themselves, '*in all their insignificance and world-altering might*[3]. While eximious at dealing with non-human nature we have not been successful at dealing with human nature itself.

We cannot afford to remain hostage to the pervasive mentality of winning and collecting. The world is not oyster to open. A scandalous vein of rationalism and materialism has grown in us which we must tame. We run as a cage in search of a bird, bringing imprisonment and the environment of dead things to the body rather than liberating the human soul which nests within it and which has very different demands. Moderns are manipulators and not lifters, they cannot be. "*[T]he torpor of their spirit, the indigent dryness of their soul, their bottomless*

---

[1] Referring to Kant's 'trostloses Ungefahr' (also translated as 'dismal reign of chance') as to how history may be defined if there were not a justified hope that the unconnected and unpredictable actions of men might not in the end bring about mankind as a politically united community together with the fully developed humanity of man. See Immanuel Kant, **"Idea for a Universal History from a Cosmopolitan Perspective,"** in Pauline Kleingeld (ed.). Toward Perpetual Peace and Other Writings on Politics, Peace, and History (New Haven: Yale University Press, 2006), IaG 8:18
[2] Edmund Burke (1730-1797), in a letter to Richard Shackleton (1726-1792), quoted in The Economist, July 24th-30th 2021 Edition, page 11
[3] Ibid.

credulity, their perverse preference for the insipid"[1] latch on and continue to lead to egregious, destructive blunders. The ability to manipulate things and to move in an object-ridden world is so pervasive and menacing that the object walls erected to protect are actually cracking leaving us exposed and foundering in the mist. The hapless rely on the lampless to lift us above the fray, more by chance than choice.   There is a perverse unmatched delight in destruction only because it is watched from a distance but no more. The coronavirus pandemic, as of yet unquenched, has highlighted how the global economic system isn't working and the stress lines are beginning to show: inequality, and the lack of resilience of the market economy being its principle symptoms.[2]

Our current circumstance possesses a property rarely taken into account but one that Sartre describes with great precision:

"When the instruments are broken and unusable, when plans are blasted and effort is meaningless, the world appears with a childlike and terrible freshness, suspended trackless in a void."[3] This void, at once threatening at once beckoning, is a chance pregnant with possibilities. Now is the hour of a new dedication,

---

[1] W.H. Auden, **"The Age of Anxiety: A Baroque Eclogue"**, Princeton University Press, Princeton, 2011, page 83

[2] Even the global climate crisis and its catastrophic threat to bio-diversity is viewed by world leaders as less an environmental and scientific issue or of ethics (the question of fairness and responsibility) and more a question of economics: who shall pay for the carbon emissions. This makes the leap into a new narrative extremely difficult.

[3] Quoted by Hannah Arendt, in her book ***Men in Dark Times***, a Harvest Book, New York, 1968, page 228.

Jean-Paul Sartre

a new severance. To ask the questions that we are afraid to ask so that the future may be rescued from its enslavement to the past.

In this thoughtless age of everyday headlines and short views and where so much is uncertain, there is one certainty.

This move from the impossible to the possible is the inaugural gesture of 'Abdu'l-Bahá (1844-1921) where pain would be forgotten and glory and honor exalted. The Apostle of the Possible, this 'teacher of God's word'[1], re-engaged with history and re-envisioned a common future to connect souls and bodies, experience and events in this irreversible movement called history, through time-space. His story will always be contemporary history; a life felt not only spatially (within

---

[1] The modest title 'Abdu'l-Bahá chose for Himself upon receiving knighthood of the British Empire on April 27th 1920 in the garden of the Military Governor's house in Haifa, Palestine, conferred in recognition for His humanitarian work in averting widespread famine due to a blockade caused by the Great War between the Allies (The Triple Entente) and the Central Powers (The Triple Alliance).

'Abdu'l-Bahá's immediate circumstance) but temporally, across time. In His capacity as a *'wise educator and reconciler of the human race'*[1].

'Abdu'l-Bahá outlives artists, men and women of letters, the deeds of businessmen, soldiers and statesmen. As for prophets and saints 'Abdu'l-Bahá outranges them all. This is not misguided canonization, nor a temptation to idolatry but to appreciate divine making, *imago Dei*, affirming not only the dignity, worth, and sacredness of God's creation, including the marvel of man, but also to understand that to be made in the image of God is to be able to perceive that which is not immediately before us and in some meaningful way bring into existence something which exists only in the imagination. How are we to understand and apply such image-bearing? Surely not by virtue alone. It is not enough that we are capable to do extraordinary things, having dominion over all things.

---

[1] Quoted in the account written by Shoghi Effendi and Lady Blomfield two months after His passing, entitled, simply, ***The Passing of 'Abdu'l-Bahá***, published by Rosenfeld Bros., Haifa, 1922

The ceremony of knighthood of 'Abdu'l-Bahá
at the residence of the British Governor
in Haifa on April 27, 1920

Nor is it sufficient to possess extraordinary characteristics, such as reason, volition, or conscience. We should see divine image as a series of demands – victory over ego's mortality, over contingency, over the anarchy of the world – of which we are incapable of imagining without a model of the absolute, a reference to human perfection in all its empirical richness and not just in uttermost abstraction. Such uniqueness lies in the model figure of 'Abdu'l-Bahá, that absolute originality which traces no predecessor and to Whom the future is already completed. He should be seen not as the primary causal agent of historic events but that He personified the principle of decisive action – the insistence, almost defiant, on acting and doing as if one is already free – emancipation from the external confines of nature. He showed us that love of divine truth can lead to the radical good.

Not to dominate the world but to better it based on the dignity of action rooted in the love of God and not in the vicious love of self or glory. To love the world and to be a part of it. Might not a 'new mythos', a world ordering itself anew, be surrounded by such a nimbus of the true absolute, not through the propositional definitions of attributes and properties, but by particulars, by telling the story of 'Abdu'l-Bahá? We really learn, as in true pedagogy, by *phronesis*, that practical, lived wisdom that works through testimonies and examples.

It is of itself a serious calamity for society that its tone of feeling, empathy, and grandeur of spirit be lowered or dulled. But the calamity becomes far more serious when, entrusted to be the new race of man, (man is the problem of our time, the problems of individuals fade away and may even be forbidden) we, the spiritual descendants of 'Abdu'l-Bahá, should remain uninstructed as to His ways, or not remain attracted enough to His person. His ability to envision alternate human reality is perhaps one of humankind's most precious gifts. Without such spiritual conditioning we shall never be able to truly educate and assimilate those whose sympathies are wider, keener and ever more liberal. They arrive in masses, eager to enter into possession of the world and gain a more vivid sense of their own life and activity. In their irrepressible development, we can remind them of a natural educator and initiator, 'Abdu'l-Bahá. Without such a figure to win their allegiance and give them direction, lawlessness may prevail.

'Abdu'l-Bahá addressed the repressed wounds and allowed these to be spoken, reclaimed and re-voiced for change (and exchange) to happen. His nature was deep and unfathomable so as to be absolute. He was able to move towards a shared and co-created narrative by a leap of imagination and *'ekstasis'*, going beyond oneself to possess a radical belief in the impossible. In His actions and demeanor 'Abdu'l-Bahá was the embodiment of a potent mixture of discourses to bear as social critique for the purpose of renewing faith. Character (hexis) <u>and</u> activity (praxis) were the impregnable marks of value in His discourse. ('Abdu'l-Bahá is not just a historical figure to revere and to admire but a phenomenon, a conceptual consummation of theology itself and its transfiguration. By this is meant that doctrinal explication and ethical transformation, both, are personified in the figure of 'Abdu'l-Bahá. No speculation anymore, nor proposition, but disposition).

Discourse is a term which cannot be seen too narrowly or used too freely. It is much more than the use of language in a social context to convey broad historical meanings. It goes beyond bridging our personal and social worlds in meaningful conversations, valuable in itself. 'Abdu'l-Bahá used discourse as a means of fellowship, citizens united together in a polis. In the constant interchange of talk (and not intimate talk in which individuals speak about themselves) we unite. There is no single voice but a plurality of voices that lead not to noise but to anthem. Hand-to-hand peacemaking cannot occur without a narrative exchange or discourse. This is the challenge. Our experience in the existential world is only done in the mode of understanding, by interpreting someone as this or that. The eye is never neutral. Nor the ear. Nor the hand. The stranger (*hostis*) before me is seen as hostile or hospitable, distant or near, cold or warm – or, more often, a composite mix calling for tactful discernment. How am I to stretch my hand? With the face of experience or the heart of innocence, always uncertain as to which human dress to wear? Should we encounter a rock in our path, we may interpret it as na obstacle, a weapon, a building brick, or material for a new work of art. *"Why to me, a stranger unknown, unheard of, should He raise that friendly hand?"* *"I cannot tell you,'* 'Abdu'l-Bahá would reply, *'but in all those upon whom I look, I see only my Father's Face."*[1] Here is a way out of our true and tried dilemma of never knowing for certain what or who the other is and also not to trust too much our figurative reading of the world. After all, is not what we make of reality already prefigured by our most basic senses and prejudices? *"When we are 'full of ourselves', cocksure, arrogant, self-sufficient and supposedly sovereign in our ego world, we cannot hearken to the stranger in others and ourselves. Only after a spiritual voiding can we retrieve the secret mystery of things, to which we are habitually blind and inattentive."*[2]

In true discourse the political importance of fellowship and the humanness peculiar to it are made manifest. There is a double duty here: to remain faithful to one's belief while remaining

---

[1] A figment composed from two separate texts. The question put is by the Unitarian Minister, Howard Colby Ives in his book, **Portals to Freedom,** page 30 and the reply is taken from **Vignettes from the Life of 'Abdu'l-Bahá**, by Annamarie Honnold, page 96.

[2] Richard Kearney, Daniël P. Veldsman, Yolande Steenkamp, Chapter 15, Across oceans: A conversation on otherness, hospitality and welcoming a strange God, in D.P. Veldsman, Y. Steenkamp (eds), **Debating Otherness with Richard Kearney: Perspectives from South Africa**, AOSIS, Cape Town, 2018.

attentive to the novelty of the foreigner's. It really is the best way to know oneself.

The shortest route from self to self is through the other. The me today to the me yesterday is because of you.[1] In dialogue with the other person, we come home to ourselves eventually. In conversation with another we travel through other worlds. We are de-worlded, as it were, by taking this detour through the imagination of the other person, the world of the other person, and we come back to ourselves, in some sense, amplified and enriched by that journey through otherness. *"'Abdu'l-Bahá voiced and made eloquent the sacred aspiration that yearns dumbly in the hearts of men. He embodied in glorious, triumphant maturity that ideal which in others lies imprisoned behind the veil.* [2]

The world does not become humane just because it is made of human beings much less because the human voice sounds in it

---

[1] Another form of conversation – that with an imagined entity, our future self – has similarly profound consequences. A strong connection to a future self, and in subsequent decision making, shows greater responsibility. Future self-continuity has been shown to achieve higher moral standards, improved health, happiness and wellbeing in general. The inspiration for the recent psychological research on the future self can be found in the writings of philosophers such as Joseph Butler, in the 18th Century. "If the self or person of today, and that of tomorrow, are not the same, but only like persons, the person of today is really no more interested in what will befall the person of tomorrow, than in what will befall any other person," Butler wrote in 1736. Refer to the recently published book by David Robson, **The Expectation Effect: How Your Mindset Can Transform Your Life**, published by Canongate in the UK (Jan 2022) and Henry Holt in the USA (Feb 2022).

[2] Quoted in in The Bahá'í World, Volume 15 (1968-1973) in commemoration of the 50 year anniversary of the passing of 'Abdu'l-Bahá.

but only when it becomes the object of discourse. However much we are affected by the things of the world, however deeply we are touched by them, they become human for us only when we can discuss them with our fellows. We humanize the world only by speaking of it. The humanness achieved in the discourse of fellowship is what is meant by the Greek word, *philanthropia*, love of man, since it manifests itself to share the world with others[1] On all occasions, in the most diverse settings, on subjects profound or not, 'Abdu'l-Bahá would free the individual from any notion of possessing truth or of being right. Both these points of view have in common the fact that neither side is prepared to sacrifice their view on humanity in case of conflict.

---

[1] This is more readily understood when we consider its opposite, misanthropy, where there is no one we care for to share the world, none worthy enough of rejoicing with in the world and nature and the cosmos. *Philia*, or friendship amongst citizens, was one of the fundamental requirements for universal wellbeing according to Aristotle.

The elimination of conflict, in all its dimensions and at all levels, was the clarion call of 'Abdu'l-Bahá even in the simplest face-to-face encounters and on matters the most prosaic.[1]

'Abdu'l-Bahá operated in two worlds and unified them – the seen and the unseen, the cognate and the incognate, the sensible and the intelligible. He was the great Unifier. The contingent and the absolute are not to be regarded as isolated spheres but drawn into common ground where the humus of faith and belief is mixed with the soil of evidence and rationality, a divine-human interplay where human action and the divine Logos, or making divine of the human and making human of the divine, operates in conjunction. Such duality was only possible because 'Abdu'l-Bahá saw experience as reality and proof of the divine as truth. In this way truth is reality and reality, truth. The comprehension of such unity discourages the blind leap of fideism – the reliance on faith, either militant or dogmatic, to disparage and denigrate reason – but also discourages the false (or misguided) assurance of certainty as established by proof, verification, demonstration

---

[1] A glimpse of this can be found in this episode narrated by the protagonist who felt an enormous guilt over smoking and for not being able to disembarrass the habit confessed his dilemma to 'Abdu'l-Bahá. After a brief interchange and where only one question was asked by the beloved Master the matter was closed: *"I was somewhat overwhelmed'*, writes the author. *'Not a dissertation on the evils of habit; not an explanation of the bad effects on health; not a summoning of my will power to overcome desire, rather a Charter of Freedom did He present to me. I did not understand but it was a great relief for somehow I knew that this was wise advice. So immediately that inner conflict was stilled and I enjoyed my smoke with no smitings of conscience. But two days after this conversation I found the desire for tobacco had entirely left me and I did not smoke again..."* Howard Colby Ives, ***Portals to Freedom***, George Ronald, Oxford, 1983, Chapter Two.

or miracle. Just as modern physics is based on the concept of the 'field', an entity that spans all space and time and tells other objects how to move, 'Abdu'l-Bahá created and lived the narrative arc or field of mimesis, where reality was reconfigured to reflect both the seen and unseen, each representing the other in how events are enacted. In the history of natural science, a brilliant leap of intuition and insight proved that the electric and magnetic fields were not two separate and distinct forces but, rather, two sides of the same coin. Electricity and magnetism are two expressions of the same, unified and invisible electromagnetic force.[1] In the 'school of God'[2] , *"...man cannot grasp the Essence of Divinity, but can, by his reasoning power, by observation, by his intuitive faculties and the revealing power of his faith, believe in God, discover the bounties of His Grace. He becometh certain that though the Divine Essence is unseen of the eye, and the existence of the Deity is intangible, yet conclusive spiritual proofs assert the existence of that unseen Reality."*[3] The analytic and the aesthetic, the material and the spiritual, the visible and the invisible, are facets of a unique synergy: God with creation, the apex of which is man. *"The spirit of man alone penetrates the realities of God and partakes of the divine bounties."*[4]

---

[1] The nineteenth century Scottish scientist, James Clerk Maxwell, is credited with the formulation of electromagnetic theory and ranks with Sir Isaac Newton and Albert Einstein for the fundamental nature of his contributions.

[2] Bahá'u'lláh, in His treatise, ***The Four Valleys.***

[3] 'Abdu'l-Bahá, ***Tablet to Dr. Auguste Forel,*** original Persian text first published Cairo 1922. This translation is taken from The Bahá'í World, Vol. XV, pp. 37–43.

[4] Abdu'l-Bahá, ***The Promulgation of Universal Peace,*** page 259

The concrete universal in the iconic image of 'Abdu'l-Bahá is thralldom. It is the only concept we can use in any objective assessment of His life. As Expounder of His Father's revelation, as Exemplar of His father's teachings, as exponent of History (the capital H is intended as the culmination of a long historical process of human reason making itself manifest), 'Abdu'l-Bahá can only really be understood in the light of thralldom, if at all.

Thralldom is the state of being in someone's power, anchored in captivity. The term *'captive in Thy Hand'* [1] gives this very idea of adherence to the Absolute and exists for the sake of what seems its very opposite – for freedom, almost an extravagance of hope and flow, the amputation from things but which anticipates the possibility of reattachment. Thralldom is a unifying power, a master condition providing stability against the shifting variety of human experience. Thralldom begins with enchantment and fealty but does not belong there. It nourishes intrinsic goodness but it is not limited to it. It is a voyage in pursuit of uncertainty, mystery and doubt – a truly scientific temperament. Thralldom is how the sacred may reveal itself to the world. It signals the traversal of the finite by the infinite, of the particular by the universal, of the mundane by the mystical, of time by eternity. For the spiritual being, thralldom or yieldedness, has to become the operative term for the ideal of everyday incarnation. We are to be totally yielded to God. When we are yielded, God will then give the gift or gifts (in the measure He alone wills) that will glorify Him as much as edify the Community under Him. If

---

[1] The phrase is from the **Tablet of Visitation**, a prayer revealed by 'Abdu'l-Bahá, and read at His Shrine. The Tablet may also be used in private prayer.

norms give beauty to all licenses and variances in our lives, such as the virtue of courtesy ('the prince of virtues'), for example, and which make possible perfect ease and freedom, thralldom empowers it.

'Abdu'l-Bahá, under His cognizance of the business and bosoms of men, and for His preference to walk 'the mystic way with practical feet'[1], might supply us with a more pragmatic, earthy, definition of thralldom, "... to *be attentive, alert and mindful, occupied with service... and ever conforming to His will.*"[2] The task of explicating the complex figure of 'Abdu'l-Bahá is impossible given that He Himself is a kind of truth. We are not just given to a 'magnetic personality' but to His kind which provides the indispensable truth for a model in altruistic motivation and selfless commitment to goodness. Even if human perfection be considered fiction, that is, it is neither true nor false, paradoxically this gives it a kind of absolute veracity and the historical facts surrounding the charismatic figure of 'Abdu'l-Bahá is proof He was neither illusion nor fiction but truth. However we wish to approach it, He created a flow of belief more valuable than an inspiring version of human fact and His utterances, inexhaustibly readable, were much more than

---

[1] Commonly attributed to Dr. David Starr Jordan, in his opening address on 'Abdu'l-Bahá during His visit to Stanford University on the morning of October 8, 1912. But this has been corrected to refer to a description appearing in a local paper at the time of 'Abdu'l-Bahá's talk at Stanford.

[2] Abdu'l-Bahá, **The Promulgation of Universal Peace,** page 355. He does, however, evoke the term thralldom explicitly and in categorical terms in this passage: *"Thralldom to the Blessed Perfection is my glorious and refulgent diadem, and servitude to all the human race my perpetual religion....No name, no title, no mention, no commendation have I, nor will ever have, except 'Abdu'l-Bahá."* [WOB] page 138.

sermonettes. His verse continues to scatter among mankind, as from an unextinguished hearth. How? As the incarnation of the ideal man? 'Abdu'l-Bahá cannot be constructed simply as the incarnation of a conceptually and exemplary pure reference to be used to specify historical significance or cultural meaning. He is not a product of sociology much less the inspiration for a new anthropology.

Rather, should we not infer from the appellation 'Mystery of God'[1] not a commingling, but a closely connected, a mutual conpenetration of the Author of Revelation [Bahá'u'lláh] to 'the unerring Interpreter of His Word' ['Abdu'l-Bahá]? A plurality of persons with no unity of divine substance, but a coalescing, a mingling, a cleaving to each other nonetheless. Does not the fact that 'Abdu'l-Bahá's sustenance is 'direct from the Fountain-head of the Bahá'í Revelation; …that His words are not equal in rank, though they possess an equal validity with the utterances of Bahá'u'lláh'[2] a suggestion, never of equality, but of unity and concordance? We are quite wrong to interpret Bahá'u'lláh's description of Him *'Who hath branched from this mighty Stock'*[3] – as an allusion that the Father is in the Son and conversely, the existential presence of divine persons in each other, but as *'wide as is the gulf that separates 'Abdu'l-Bahá from Him Who is the Source of an independent Revelation'*, there is nevertheless one and the same motion, one impulse, which is

---

[1] An expression which Bahá'u'lláh Himself had chosen to designate His Son. See Shoghi Effendi, ***World Order of Bahá'u'lláh***, Wilmette, US Bahá'í Publishing Trust, 1991, page 134.
[2] Ibid.
[3] Ibid.

not to be observed in any created nature. For the Father is the Father of someone, i.e., of the Son; and the Son is the Son of someone, i.e., of the Father. To quote Thomas Aquinas, *"…the Father is by essence in the Son, for the Father is his essence and communicates his essence to the Son, doing this not by any transmutation of himself; then from this follows, since the essence of the Father is in the Son, that the Father is in the Son. Similarly, since the Son is also his essence, it follows that the Son is in the Father, being in him his essence."*[1] Much as we would like to drowse in special perspectives of individual interpretation and speculation, however, it is to the theology of the word, that unassailable foundation of dispensation, that we must turn to and it is this, *"…His Holiness… the Abhá Beauty (Bahá'u'lláh)…is the supreme Manifestation of God and the Day-Spring of His most divine Essence. All others are servants unto Him…."*[2] Our steps inevitably return to a difficult beginning and we are caught in a hard chasm: to overestimate 'Abdu'l-Bahá is as reprehensible as underestimating Him. In this oddest and most hidden of all places 'Abdu'l-Bahá is revealed unknown. We are preserved, however, in our limited minds by these insolate words: *"That 'Abdu'l-Bahá is not a Manifestation of God, that He gets His light, His inspiration and sustenance direct from the Fountain-head of the Bahá'í Revelation; that He reflects even as*

---

[1] This is, of course, taken out of a different context from Aquinas' **Summa Theologiae**, where he expounds on the circuminsession of all the Divine Persons, *circumincessio* in Latin, but it was felt appropriate given its relevance to the idea contained in John's Gospel where Jesus says: *I am in the Father and the Father in me.* (John 14:11), for us to better appreciate the idea of pure emanation ('Abdu'l-Bahá) from the glory of the Almighty (Bahá'u'lláh).

[2] 'Abdu'l-Bahá, quoted in Shoghi Effendi, "**The World Order of Bahá'u'lláh**: Selected Letters", rev. ed. (Wilmette: Bahá'í Publishing Trust, 1982), page 61

a clear and perfect Mirror the rays of Bahá'u'lláh's glory, and does not inherently possess that indefinable yet all-pervading reality the exclusive possession of which is the hallmark of Prophethood; that His words are not equal in rank, though they possess an equal validity with the utterances of Bahá'u'lláh;"[1] – are imponderable truths mantled in mist but which offer a dismissing path to that point in our knowledge where the longing to touch this magical marvel never rests or leaves us.

*Shoghi Effendi, eldest grandson
of 'Abdu'l-Bahá*

---

[1] Shoghi Effendi, 'Abdu'l-Bahá, quoted in Shoghi Effendi, "**The World Order of Bahá'u'lláh**: Selected Letters", rev. ed. (Wilmette: Bahá'í Publishing Trust, 1982), page 64

PART TWO

HISTORY OF THE FUTURE

In the fairest traditions of understanding society to make it better, of an instinctive, forward looking universalism of a non-political nature (refer to page 35), and to see justice prevail in every domain of human society, the Bahá'í Faith of which 'Abdu'l-Bahá was, in his lifetime, its most eminent practitioner, is already writing the future. In service to mankind, this nascent Faith, now well into its second century, is guiding us out of *the whirlwind of insincerity and selfishness'* which, if unchecked, shall destroy civilization.

Whither our direction, the direction of social and economic development, the sense of community and the ethos of giving? And what to do? These questions imply looking into the future, so far as this is possible - a risky, frequently a disappointing, but also a necessary activity. And prediction rests on inferences about the future from the past. The historical context of 'Abdu'l-Bahá (Part One) provided us with many lessons. Conversely, these move us closer to the future. What we read in Part One belongs to yesterday. What we are now about to say in Part Two may well belong to today and tomorrow.

We are all rooted in the past—by our families, communities, nations and even of personal memory—but now I am tempted to say 'more than ever'. Our conscious human action (learning, memory and experience), constantly confronts the past, present and future to reproduce, change and transform. It is innate and required of us. And as humanity matures so does unpredictability loom less large. While uncertainty is omnipresent it is to areas where uncertainty appears to be greatest that we must concentrate and not where it is least. Meteorologists are not needed to tell us that spring follows winter. We are intellectually better prepared today to concentrate our efforts more effectively for desired outcomes and this makes the function of prognosis less unpopular. The desire to act and the power to will are the twin, intertwined concepts at stake. [1] We have never, in our history as homo sapiens, been better placed collectively to alter the future. Returning to the metaphor of the meteorologist, we don't want to know anymore when to stock up with suntan lotion but when to create sunshine. Whatever the future fate of our history, may it not be short and precarious.

In 1921, the Formative Period of the Bahá'í Era had begun and '...*the Administration of Bahá'u'lláh's invincible Faith was born...The Will and Testament of 'Abdu'l-Bahá unveiled its character, reaffirmed its basis, supplemented its principles, asserted its indispensability, and enumerated its chief institutions...* " [2]

The starting point in this new panorama is our own life which cannot be left unexamined nor conveniently herded under some rubric. Immanence, or meaning embedded in the human, so called lived reality, is the central theme to watch and which 'Abdu'l-Bahá provides such extraordinarily rich, passionate and complex treatment. Not to discover any preconscious history or

---

[1] Not to be confused with Nietzsche's concept of the will to power. An altogether different proposition. We are not inferring the desire for domination but the affirmation to grow and overcome together.

[2] Shoghi Effendi, "***The World Order of Bahá'u'lláh***: Selected Letters", rev. ed. (Wilmette: Bahá'í Publishing Trust, 1982), page 89

natal attachment to the world but how to interpret our lives and consequently to change it. Action after action, and insight after insight, 'Abdu'l-Bahá brings us to the edge of hope where we may find reunion. He recaptured wholeness through the resurrecting power of fellowship. No death is so awful as that of fellowship. God Himself would mourn it. *"Fellowship, fellowship! Love, love! Unity, unity!—so that the power of the Bahá'í Cause may appear and become manifest in the world of existence."*[1].

June 29, 1912, 'Abdu'l-Baha at the Unity Feast in West Englewood, New Jersey, Grounds of Roy Wilhelm's Property Teaneck, New Jersey

It is the power of the Cause which gives us the sentiment that wish may be fulfilled – or hope. To live without hope is to live

---

[1] 'Abdu'l-Bahá, **Tablets of the Divine Plan**, Wilmette, US Bahá'í Publishing Trust, 1993, page 30.

in despair. We see daily signs of progress which makes us hopeful: the unlimited freedom and capacity to innovate, global interaction and cooperation, the unification of the different branches of science, discoveries of both the invisible and the visible thanks to the power of computing and artificial intelligence, the removal of pain and the elimination of disease, and much more. The process of discovery, however, proceeds much faster than the capacity for society to reinvent and reorganize itself. Humanity is on course but is in urgent need of inspired guidance and unification. Hope must be centered on the 'Universal Reality', a morality of response and responsibility which is rooted in genuine love of humanity and of the universe. This is the best hope because there is divine grace in it. Without divine grace the promise will not be fulfilled and to be open to divine grace requires humble *kenosis*, whereby the self is emptied of will to become receptive to a higher will.

Visions of ideal societies have recurred throughout history but such societies were nearly always placed in an irretrievable past. The paradise of milk and honey of which human beings dreamed – a land of perpetual peace and abundance – belonged in religion and mythology rather than history or science. Yet by the end of the 19th century, the fiction of an ideal society had been turned into a realizable human condition. Already in the second half of the 18th century, Rousseau was writing of an egalitarian society as if something of the kind had once existed – a move repeated by Marx and Engels in their theory of primitive communism, which they believed could be recreated at a higher level.

Friedrich Engels   *Karl Marx*

Much earlier, the Renaissance humanist, Thomas More had given us a glimpse of utopia which ever since has become a dominant political legend.

What is the normal course of history? So-called primitive cultures understood that history runs in cycles, with civilizations rising and falling much as the seasons come and go – a view of things echoed in Aristotle and the Roman historians. The rise of monotheism changed the picture, so that history came to be seen as an unfolding drama, an intelligible process – a story with a heroic beginning, a formative middle and a redemptive, golden end. Either way, no one believed that history could be governed by human will. It was fate, God or mere chaos that ruled human events. Given the ghastly record of utopian politics in the 20th century, thinkers and dreamers of all stripes never tire of declaring that all they want is improvement. They assume that the advances of the past are now permanent and new ones can simply be added on. But if one thinks society today is like all others have been – deeply flawed and highly fragile – it is clear that improvement can't be inherited in this way. Sooner or later, past advances are sure to be lost, as the societies that have inherited them decline and fail. Law is not enough to deal with the many questions that are to be addressed. Nobody lives or dies for abstract laws and constitutions. People need narratives, traditions, stories of belonging, because what the heart does not feel, it cannot share. The impossible can only work in terms of such a spiritual wager, a leap of imagination and faith. Politics cannot legislate for that.

Believers in improvement, the scattered Bahá'í nation inhabits many lands – places where what has been achieved in the past can be handed on into an indefinite future. The human impulse to dream up and believe imaginary places and then see them to be real is as strong as it has ever been because 'Abdu'l-Bahá proved His Father's doctrine to the pulse so that we may see it as palpable and solid. He engaged in reflection which forces us to reflect. His was the area of happening of the 'reflexive faith' (i.e. conscious) as described by Kant - a serene and luminous region of truth where all may meet and expatiate in common above the din and turmoil of everyday life. To love the world is to act in it. The motive of human action is love of the world. Wheels are turning and we cannot stand still to avoid that mankind, disgarlanded of genius, character and originality, forever remain an object of ridicule and contempt.

The appearance of 'Abdu'l-Bahá, this 'most perfect bounty', this 'most great favor' conferred upon men, provides an important and necessary function – that of incarnating the ideal. In this way we are spared the assumption of ever having a literal and immediate possession of divine mystery or alterity. This would force us to ignore our finitude. The idealist presumption that we possess God, that we can comprehend God, and that human consciousness can actually identify with absolute consciousness is a temptation which has, thankfully, been removed. We are saved by the figurative '*as*' in 'Abdu'l-Bahá's intriguing exhortation – '*Be as I am*'[1]. Not in the fictional laboratory of '*as if*' where all things are possible and anything can be imagined with freedom and impunity but in the conjunction '*as*'. 'As' is figuration; 'as if' is fiction. We have in 'Abdu'l-Bahá a sacred Giver of life, a superhuman person in a profanely finite world. Faith needs both flesh and imagination. (As Aristotle put it in his *De Anima*, 'flesh is a medium ('metaxu') not just an organ). The creedal is composed of both the carnal and the revealed poetic. 'Abdu'l-Bahá showed us how the empirical seeing-as and the religious believing-as are indispensable in any imagination of

---

[1] "*...Look at me, look at Me, follow Me, be as I am; take no thought for yourselves or your lives, whether ye eat or whether we sleep, whether we are comfortable, whether we are well or ill, whether ye are with friends or foes, whether ye receive praise or blame; for all of these things we must care not at all. Look at Me and be as I am; ye must die to yourselves and to the world, so shall ye be born again and enter the Kingdom of Heaven. Behold a candle and how it gives its light. It weeps its life away drop by drop in order to give forth its flame of light.*" Quoted in the notes of May Maxwell, the mother of Ruhiyyih Khánum, from an 1898 pilgrimage, entitled, **An Early Pilgrimage**, and published by George Ronald in 1917.

human reality - but an imagination that doesn't go on holiday, where anything goes and all is permitted.

Although 'Abdu'l-Bahá Himself was an exile (ever since the tender age of nine)[1], it is really we who are in exile, unable to find another or think of another. The term exile surely includes every kind of estrangement or displacement, from the physical and geographical to the spiritual. An "ontological exile" is our concern, a spiritual displacement, an uprootedness, a perpetual wandering. Humanity is dislocated from both its point of origin as well as its destination. Where is this place that we must be, stuck in thereness, lost? Our homelands have become foreign lands. But the exilic condition, *"the rift forced between a human being and a native place, between the self and its true home"*[2] is not incurable. The outward fear brings inner peace. Hellish trees can co-exist with flame trees (flamboyant) that shelter us – Eden is not fatally compromised nor doomed. Human divinity and human corruption are destined to live side by side but we can only read them by mentally turning the page and allow the forceful negative psychological insight of one place to explain the idealism of the other place and not to cancel it. Virtues are meaningless without the evils they correct. *"Unless one accepts*

---

[1] In the bitter winter, on January 12th 1853 to be precise, a very young 'Abdu'l-Bahá in the company of His illustrious Father and other members of the Holy Family, set out from their native land, Persia, to begin the three month's journey to Baghdad. "[T]he first stage of a memorable and life-long exile…" See **God Passes By**, Chapter VII.

[2] Edward W. Said, from his posthumous book **Reflections on Exile and Other Essays**, published by Harvard University Press, 2000.

dire vicissitudes he will not attain"[1] is 'Abdu'l-Bahá's incontrovertible injunction. He goes further, and points to the wisdom of world crises: *"Chaos and confusion are daily increasing in the world. They will attain such intensity as to render the frame of mankind unable to bear them. Then will men be awakened and become aware that religion is the impregnable stronghold and the manifest light of the world, and its laws, exhortations and teachings the source of life on earth."*[2]

The centenary of the passing of 'Abdu'l-Bahá discloses once again His era-defining odyssey - *ecce homo,* a last living prose which God wrote with the secret signature of things, 'a seer among blind men'. The world to which we must return can never really be the same. But the healing, the conviction that the *genus homo* is not set in its ways, is always one day at a time, never once and for all. *'Little by little, day by day'* (*'Kam Kam Ruz bih Ruz,* in Farsi')[3]– is 'Abdu'l-Bahá''s very own counselling on how to attain the promise of a new surplus, a new fulfilling. But while life has no end it has a definite beginning and we must make sure that the good our hands do well exceeds to what the body may wrest. There is no high road to Damascus but nor is it a lost Armada. From 'Abdu'l-Bahá's immense, prodigious and beatified handiwork, resourcefully distilled by Balyuzi's

---

[1] 'Abdu'l-Bahá,, ***'Abdu'l-Bahá in London***, UK Bahá'í Publishing Trust, 1982, page 120.
[2] 'Abdu'l-Bahá, quoted in the ***Compilation on Peace***, by the Research Department of the Universal House of Justice, Bahá'í World Centre, August 1985, page 12.
[3] 'Abdu'l-Bahá, in ***Bahá'í World,*** Volume 12: 704

apothegm "*...a life, abundant, spacious, immeasurable*"[1] there is a first lesson to be learnt to prevent the disintegration of the world or the dissolution of those values which are supreme, absolute and, therefore, non-earthly. To be a true agent for change we must move incessantly between pragmatic, lasting altruism and self-effacement, mirroring the divine. These two poles characterize the interiority and grandeur of human agency. Otherwise we shall continue to polish imaginary fragments shored against our ruins. 'Abdu'l-Bahá came not to shame us but to make us more lofty. He does not allow us to despair but encourages a complex hope sustained by service to the cause of humanity through His Father's message of love and brotherhood. Here is an extraordinary modern story where utterance is permanence and the movement it gave form to has, at its molten heart, the image of servitude – an image nested in memory and renewal, continuity and rupture - dispassionate and compelling.

---

[1] Hasan M. Balyuzi, `*Abdu'l-Bahá: The Centre of the Covenant* ⌐
GR Publishing, UK, 1971, page 3.

Portrait of 'Abdu'l-Bahá taken in Paris,
France, October 1911

ACKNOWLEDGMENTS

This short composition is not a single authorial voice but of many voices, from high and low alike, from prophets and sages, from the known to the unknown, so as to invite contemplation and to make room for a new faith while not denying the knowledge that leads to it. When trying to familiarize the reader with the person of 'Abdu'l-Bahá (or Servant of the Glory, in Arabic) there is really no recourse but to be helplessly unoriginal. How else to revitalize a majestic and towering historical figure who blends *"the incompatible characteristics of a human nature and superhuman knowledge and perfection...*?[1] I have, therefore, adopted (and adapted) the intellectual output of many, unabashedly, and maybe too freely - a self-confessed master of borrowing -by using their arguments to build mine. This essay and the movement of its parts, therefore, falls into an indistinct zone, difficult and uncertain.

My many sincere thanks to many an enjoyable coterie of talent, advice and command. My notorious untutorable sensibilities have been firmly and patiently chiseled by an able, discerning and meticulous battle-hardened reviewer, Martha Schweitz, who leads the Office of Review at the US Bahá'í National Center, and whose insightful suggestions to the text

---

[1] Shoghi Effendi, *The World Order of Bahá'u'lláh*, BPT, 1974, page 61

eliminated the polemic and the problematic to allow a final revision to be formally approved for publishing. I have received invaluable support and encouragement from people closest and dearest to me: my wife and guiding spirit, Neda, loving advisor, and eminent defender; my sons Shayan and Arman, my creative daughter-in-law Vitoria and daughter Shiva who, together with her dear husband, Adib Shaikhzadeh, went even further than what may be expected from next of kin. My older brother Shahab strongly encouraged me to plunge into the world of self-publishing unobstructed by the dread of financial risk and other concerns. This undertaking was a healing and rewarding experience, nonetheless, especially when aided and abetted by a master practitioner, Professor Boris Handal, in distant Australia, who lovingly and generously guided me and with his practical skill and extensive publishing and writing experience, never patronizing always encouraging, and who allowed me to stay the course and navigate safely to port. Warmest thanks to him. On the crucial task of book formatting and design I am forever indebted to Ruth Shafa for her artful and assiduous trouble in bringing the manuscript into a most pleasing fruition. Her patience, formidable experience and enviable goodwill was the garnish of this entire collective enterprise – what a delight to work with! In this vein, I must also include the invaluable and engaging assistance of Ana Beatriz Pereira Melo, an English major undergraduate, whose tasteful and sensitive selection of photographs only added flavor to the finished product and to the experience itself not to mention her tedious task of organizing the bibliography. Last but not least, to my mother, Shafiqeh, I offer this modest gift of a book for her upcoming 100th birthday

– a life of service well lived and whose precepts convey the instructions I shall ever need, namely, the ambition to be forgetful of self and ever-mindful of that which is God's.

All human endeavor becomes special when guided by the trust, wisdom, and dedicated experience of a spiritually learned individual. I was most fortunate to have had the gift of friendship of Dr. Iraj Ayman since my London days in the mid-nineteen seventies and to whom I owe the inscrutable joy of learning swayed between extremes of ecstasy and despair in unapprehended, uplifting journeys of inspiration. Him I must truly regard as an indispensable counselor and father to anyone hoping to craft literary material as a function of religious belief.

'Abdu'l-Bahá. *Foundations of World Unity*. Wilmette: Bahá'í Publishing Trust. (1979)

__________. *The Bahá'í World, Volume 12*. Wilmette: Bahá'í Publishing Trust. (1956)

———. *Tablets of the Divine Plan*. Wilmette: Bahá'í Publishing Trust. (1993)

__________ *Tablet to Dr. Auguste Forel*. Cairo: Sa'adat Press. (1922)

———. *The Promulgation of Universal Peace*. Wilmette: Bahá'í Publishing Trust. (1982)

———. *Tablet of Visitation*. Wilmette: Bahá'í Publishing Trust. (1991)

__________. *'Abdu'l-Bahá in London*. London: Bahá'í Publishing Trust. (1982)

———. *The Bahá'í World, Volume 12*. Haifa: Bahá'í World Centre. (1981)

__________Quoted in *Compilation on Peace*, Research Department of the Universal House of Justice. Haifa: Bahá'í World Centre. (1985)

Aquinas, Thomas. *Summa Theologiae*. New York: Benziger Bros. (1947)

Arendt, Hannah. *Men in Dark Times*. New York: Harcourt, Brace & World. (1968)

Auden, W. H. *The Age of Anxiety*. Princeton: Princeton University Press. (2011)

Bahá'u'lláh. *The Four Valleys*. Wilmette: Bahá'í Publishing Trust. (1991)

Balyuzi, Hasan M. *'Abdu'l-Bahá: The Centre of the Covenant of Bahá'u'lláh*. Oxford: George Ronald. (1971)

Bell, Clive. *Civilization*. London: Chatto & Windus. (1928)

Burke, Edmund. *Letter to Richard Shackleton*. Cambridge: Cambridge University Press. (1730–1797)

Chesterton, G. K. *Orthodoxy*. San Francisco: Ignatius Press. (1995)

Effendi, Shoghi. *The Passing of 'Abdu'l-Bahá*. Haifa: Rosenfeld Bros. (1922)

______________. *The World Order of Bahá'u'lláh: Selected Letters*. Wilmette: Bahá'í Publishing Trust. (1982)

______________. *God Passes By*. Wilmette: Bahá'í Publishing Trust. (1974)

Eliot, T. S. *The Waste Land*. New York: Boni and Liveright. (1922)

Ferguson, Niall. *The Ascent of Money: A Financial History of the World*. New York: Penguin Press. (2008)

Harrod, R. F. *The Life of John Maynard Keynes*. London: Macmillan. (1951)

Hobsbawm, Eric. *The Age of Extremes: A History of the World, 1914–1991*. New York: Pantheon Books. (1995)

———. *The Age of Capital: 1848–1875*. London: Weidenfeld & Nicolson. (1975)

Honnold, Annamarie. *Vignettes from the Life of 'Abdu'l-Bahá*. Oxford: George Ronald. (1982)

Ives, Howard Colby. *Portals to Freedom*. Oxford: George Ronald. (1983)

John 14:11. *New Testament, The Holy Bible, KJV*.

Joyce, James. *Ulysses*. Paris: Sylvia Beach. (1922)

Kafka, Franz. *Die Zürauer Aphorismen*. Berlin: Verlag Die Schmiede. (1931)

Kant, Immanuel ed. *"Idea for a Universal History from a Cosmopolitan Perspective,"* in Pauline Kleingeld (ed.). Toward Perpetual Peace and Other Writings on Politics, Peace, and History. New Haven: Yale University Press, 2006

Kearney, Richard, Daniël P. Veldsman, and Yolande Steenkamp, eds. *Debating Otherness with Richard Kearney: Perspectives from South Africa*. Cape Town: African Sun Media. (2018)

Keynes, John Maynard. *The General Theory of Employment, Interest and Money*. London: Macmillan. (1935)

Maxwell, May. *An Early Pilgrimage*. London: George Ronald. (1917)

Nietzsche, Friedrich W., *Gay Science*, London (1910)

Owen, Wilfred. *Poems*. London: Chatto & Windus. (1920)

Perry, Marvin; Berg, Matthew; and Krukones, James. *Sources of European History Since 1900*. Boston: Cengage Learning. (2011)

Phelps, Myron Henry, and Bahiyyih Khánum. *Life and Teachings of Abbas Effendi*. New York: Putnam. (1903)

Piketty, Thomas. *Capital in the Twenty-First Century*. Cambridge: Harvard University Press. (2014)

Robson, David. *The Expectation Effect: How Your Mindset Can Transform Your Life*. New York: Henry Holt. (2018)

Said, Edward W. *Reflections on Exile and Other Essays*. Cambridge: Harvard University Press. (2000)

Smith, Adam. *The Theory of Moral Sentiments*. London: A. Millar. (1790)

Toynbee, Arnold. *A Study of History*. London: Oxford University Press. (1952)

Ward, Alan. *239 Days: 'Abdu'l-Bahá's Journey in America*. Wilmette: Bahá'í Publishing Trust. (1979)

Wilson, Woodrow. Quoted in *Prologue Magazine. America Enters the Great War*. Washington: National Archives. (2017)

www.ingramcontent.com/pod-product-compliance
Lightning Source LLC
Chambersburg PA
CBHW050040040726
47599CB00015B/1762